●=ON-THE-JOB ORIENTATION AND TRAINING

A Practical Guide To Enhanced Performance

Larry R. Smalley

Jossey-Bass
Pfeiffer
San Francisco

RICHARD
CHANG
ASSOCIATES

Printed in the United States of America

Published by

350 Sansome Street, 5th Floor
San Francisco, California 94104-1342
(415) 433-1740; Fax (415) 433-0499
(800) 274-4434; Fax (800) 569-0443

Visit our website at: www.pfeiffer.com

Printing   10   9   8   7   6   5   4   3   2   1

ACKNOWLEDGMENTS

About The Author

Larry Smalley, a Vice President for Richard Chang Associates, Inc., is a highly experienced, results-oriented human resources professional. His broad management background and demonstrated success in diverse environments allowed him to develop a proficiency in linking human resources systems to strategic business goals. He has particular expertise in organizational assessment and design, competency based selection and training systems, performance management implementation, compensation and incentive systems, and employee relations.

The author would like to acknowledge the support of the entire team of professionals at Richard Chang Associates, Inc. for their contribution to the guidebook development process. In addition, special thanks are extended to the many client organizations who have helped us shape the practical ideas and proven methods shared in this guidebook.

Additional Credits

Editors:	Sarah Ortlieb Fraser and Scott Rimmer
Reviewers:	Richard Chang, Jim Greeley, and P. Keith Kelly
Graphic Layout:	Doug Westfall, Jacqueline Westfall, and Christina Slater
Cover Design:	John Odam Design Associates

PREFACE

The 1990's have already presented individuals and organizations with some very difficult challenges to face and overcome. So who will have the advantage as we move toward the year 2000 and beyond?

The advantage will belong to those with a commitment to continuous learning. Whether on an individual basis or as an entire organization, one key ingredient to building a continuous learning environment is *The Practical Guidebook Collection* brought to you by the Publications Division of Richard Chang Associates, Inc.

After understanding the future *"learning needs"* expressed by our clients and other potential customers, we are pleased to publish *The Practical Guidebook Collection*. These guidebooks are designed to provide you with proven, *"real-world"* tips, tools, and techniques— on a wide range of subjects—that you can apply in the workplace and/or on a personal level immediately.

Once you've had a chance to benefit from *The Practical Guidebook Collection*, please share your feedback with us. We've included a brief *Evaluation and Feedback Form* at the end of the guidebook that you can fax to us at (714) 727-7007.

With your feedback, we can continuously improve the resources we are providing through the Publications Division of Richard Chang Associates, Inc.

Wishing you successful reading,

Richard Y. Chang
President and CEO
Richard Chang Associates, Inc.

TABLE OF CONTENTS

1. **Introduction** 1
   Why Read This Guidebook?
   Who Should Read This Guidebook?
   When And How To Use It

2. **Expectations And Disappointments** 9
   Case Example: Frank James

3. **The Need For A Plan** 21
   A Test To Rate Job Orientation
   The Importance Of An Orientation Plan

4. **Critical Lead-Up To Day One** 29
   A Sharing Of Responsibilities And Roles
   The Organization's "Orientation Survival Kit"
   Your Departmental Orientation Checklist
   Key Questions To Ask When Planning An Employee's First Day
   Frank's Meeting With The Human Resources Department

5. **Day One: Survival** 45
   May I Present . . .
   Where Am I?
   How's It Going?

6. **Week One: Coming Up For Air** 55
   Key Questions For The First Week
   The Orientation Plan
   Week In Review
   Janet's First Week

7.   Month One: Looking Around **63**
Key Questions For The First Month
Monitoring And Adjusting The Orientation Plan
Janet's First Month

8.   Six Months: Getting There **71**
Key Questions For The First Six Months
Monitoring And Adjusting The Orientation Plan
Janet's First Six Months

9.   Twelve Months: You've Arrived! **77**
Key Questions For The First Year
Monitoring And Adjusting The Orientation Plan
Janet's First Year

10.   Ongoing Training: Your Responsibility **81**
Frank's Insight
Understanding The On-The-Job Training Process
Sample Training Needs / Objects Matrix
Clarifying Training Needs And Objectives
Selecting Behavioral Outcomes
Seven General Training Methods

11.   Summary **95**

Appendix **99**

"Trainees learn only 16 percent of what they read; 20 percent of what they see; 30 percent of what they are told; 50 percent of what they see and are told and 70 percent of what they see, are told and respond to; and 90 percent of what they do."

Joe L. Whitley

CHAPTER ONE

INTRODUCTION

On-the-Job Orientation and Training is designed to assist managers and supervisors in providing new employees valuable information about their organizations and jobs.

The aim of orientation is to help a new employee make a smooth, positive adjustment to the workplace. To do this, you need a well-planned and executed orientation program that will:

> ☞ reduce the employee's anxiety level
>
> ☞ foster a positive attitude toward the organization
>
> ☞ answer questions not handled at the time of hiring
>
> ☞ reinforce or establish realistic job expectations

The goal of on-the-job training, whether for new or ongoing employees, is to ensure there is a precise match between the requirements of the job and the skills and competencies of employees.

Orientation enables the new employee to gain familiarity with the work environment and to acquire a sense of belonging that will build a commitment to the organization. The main objectives for on-the-job orientation are to:

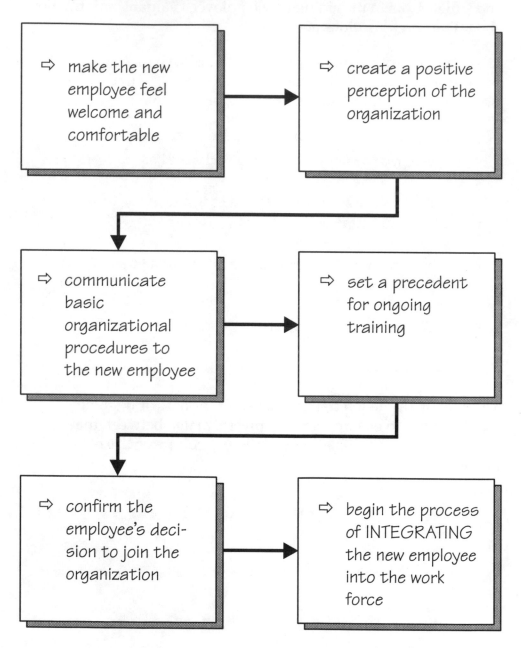

⇨ make the new employee feel welcome and comfortable

⇨ create a positive perception of the organization

⇨ communicate basic organizational procedures to the new employee

⇨ set a precedent for ongoing training

⇨ confirm the employee's decision to join the organization

⇨ begin the process of INTEGRATING the new employee into the work force

Why Read This Guidebook?

As a manager or supervisor, one of your most important roles is to direct the efforts of the people you hire. A new employee's first few days, weeks, and months are crucial to your success as an effective leader. During this formative time, the employee is impressionable and has the highest expectations. What happens as a new employee gains a *"first impression"* affects his or her attitude, which in turn affects your job. Thus, the need for new employee orientation, followed by ongoing training.

To understand the importance of first impressions, consider what happened to Roger Thompson. Roger had always dreamed of taking a vacation to Paris, and last summer he was finally able to do so. On the flight from New York to Paris, he went over his itinerary, making mental notes of his expectations.

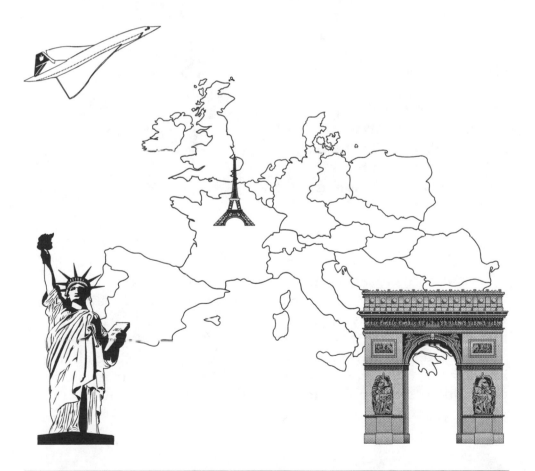

Roger arrived at his hotel in Paris at 10:00 P.M. He retired for the night to recuperate from the exhausting flight. The next morning he woke up, ready to spend the day at the Louvre.

He bought a ticket on the Metro and boarded a standing-room only subway car. While on the Metro, he double-checked his wallet to make sure he had enough cash for a leisurely lunch at one of Paris' fashionable cafés. He was angry to discover his wallet missing, along with all his credit cards. Realizing that he had been pickpocketed, Roger looked at his fellow passengers with suspicion. He got off the Metro at the next stop, shaking his head in disbelief that his dream vacation was now ruined. As he walked back to his hotel, he couldn't help but feel negatively about Paris and Parisians.

Likewise, if a new employee has a bad experience during the first impressionable days on the job, those negative feelings can cast a *"dark cloud"* over that employee's attitude. In the worst case, the new employee might feel so slighted and discouraged that he or she quits before really beginning. Then you have to hire another person, wasting valuable time and recruiting resources you already spent. Even if the new employee doesn't quit after getting off to a bad start, he or she could develop a negative attitude that could pose a long-term problem for you and your organization.

The problems associated with the loss of a new employee because of a poor orientation need not occur. A good orientation can win the employee over to his or her job and enable you to develop that person as a valuable, creative, and productive part of your team.

This guidebook will help you successfully develop on-the-job orientation and ongoing training for new and existing employees. You will find examples to help you create dynamic programs. After reading this guidebook, you will know exactly what steps to take, when to take them, and how to implement them.

Who Should Read This Guidebook?

Any manager or supervisor who routinely hires professional, technical, and nonexempt employees should use this guidebook. Human resources personnel should use this guidebook when planning and implementing departmental or divisional orientation plans. In fact, anyone involved in any aspect of new employee orientation and training will find this guidebook extremely helpful.

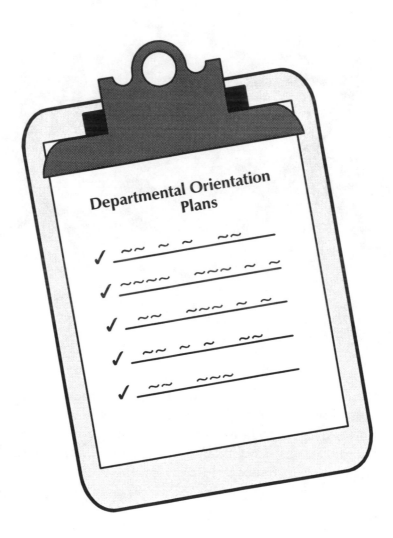

When And How To Use It

Use this material when you're building an orientation plan for your department. Alternatively, this material is beneficial to use when you're hiring a new employee or a current employee is taking on new responsibilities. This guidebook will help you cover all elements of on-the-job orientation and training. It will enable you to understand your role in the process, and help you work with human resources personnel to effectively integrate new employees into your organization.

An important feature of this guidebook is its flexibility. Since every organization is unique, this flexible guidebook can help you prepare an orientation and training plan specifically tailored to your organization's requirements. The questions, checklists, and examples provided throughout this guidebook can be easily adapted into existing organizational plans or can help you form an entirely new plan.

And if your focus is on training only, Chapter Ten and the Appendix present valuable ideas and tools you can use to create and implement effective training plans. Either way, this guidebook is an invaluable resource for creating an effective orientation and training program for your new employees.

Let's turn to a case example that we will be using throughout this guidebook to demonstrate how to develop and implement an on-the-job orientation and training plan.

EXPECTATIONS AND DISAPPOINTMENTS

Case Example: Frank James

Frank James tossed and turned all night as he anxiously imagined what his first day would be like at his new job at Metasoft Corporation. Frank was a seasoned manager and an extraordinary technical writer. He had spent 20 years of his professional life in high-tech companies, and had a reputation for developing innovative ways to explain the use of sophisticated software products. Over the years, he had managed the development and writing of hundreds of product manuals and computer-based training products.

Metasoft, an organization that creates specialty software for the healthcare industry, hired Frank for a fresh perspective in their Product Documentation Department. His mission at Metasoft was to do whatever was necessary—including the hiring of many new professionals—to create exemplary product reference and training materials. This new challenge thrilled Frank, and he looked forward to his first day at Metasoft.

Product Documentation Department

Although Frank's alarm would ring at 6 A.M. on the day he started at Metasoft, he couldn't wait to get going, so he was up early making notes of specific questions to ask during his orientation activities. He arrived in the lobby of Metasoft promptly at 7:45 A.M.—bright, shining, and raring to go. When he introduced himself to the receptionist, she greeted him with a blank stare and responded, *"Oh, I didn't think anyone new was starting today!"*

The receptionist asked Frank to have a seat while she phoned the Human Resources Department for any information about this new employee. In overhearing the receptionist's call, it was apparent to Frank that the Human Resources Department wasn't aware he was starting today either. Somewhat embarrassed by the situation, the receptionist offered Frank a cup of coffee and assured him that someone would be with him shortly.

Frank accepted the coffee and began to wonder if he had shown up on the wrong day. At 8:15 A.M., Joanne, a human resources representative, came to the lobby to introduce herself. She apologized for the mix-up and said they were getting his paperwork together and it would be ready in a few more minutes. Frank let out a sigh of relief—this was the right day after all!

Frank watched the hands of the clock rotate, and at 9:25 A.M. Joanne finally came back and escorted him to an empty, windowless conference room. After offering him another cup of coffee, Joanne gave Frank a thick packet of forms and left him alone to complete them. Filling out forms ranked just below root canal surgery on Frank's list of things to avoid, but he gritted his teeth and started plowing through them. As he finished the last tedious form, he figured the worst was now over, and he looked forward to a more positive experience for the rest of the day.

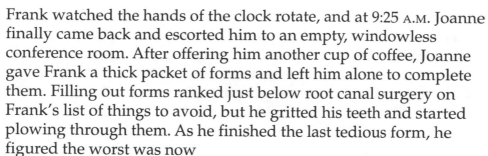

Much to his surprise, upon giving the completed forms to the receptionist, she told him that he now needed to go off-site to a health clinic. At the health clinic he would need to complete some medical forms, and have a physical examination as part of the process of enrolling in the organization's health insurance plan. She gave Frank directions to the health clinic, and said he needed to leave immediately since he would need to be back at 1 P.M. to attend the Monday staff meeting for all department managers in the Product Development Division.

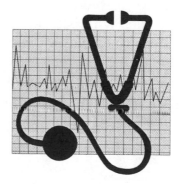

At the health clinic, Frank was greeted with yet another stack of forms. As before, he managed to fill them out rather quickly. The clinic's receptionist said they would call his name when it was his turn to go in for the physical exam. Around 11:30 A.M., a nurse ushered him into an exam room for a brief physical. The doctor commented that he seemed to be in pretty good shape for a middle-aged man, gave Frank another form, and then directed him down the hallway to have a blood sample drawn.

12 Noon

By now it was noon, and Frank just wanted to return to Metasoft. He became annoyed when he saw the line for drawing blood. Several people were ahead of him, and he realized that there was no way he would make it to his 1 P.M. meeting on time; in fact, he would probably miss it completely. By this time, the day's events had started to affect Frank. He mumbled under his breath, *"This is just great! I'm going to miss my first meeting at Metasoft, and there's nothing I can do about it. I don't even have a phone number to let the Vice President of Product Development know why I won't be able to attend the meeting."*

Frank finally left the health clinic parking lot at 1:45 P.M. He sped to Metasoft, parked his car, and sprinted to the lobby. Although he was slightly out of breath, he composed himself and calmly asked the receptionist how to get to the Product Development Division staff meeting. He made his way, with occasional help, through a maze of hallways to the correct conference room. Just as he was about to enter, people began leaving the conference room.

PRODUCT DEVELOPMENT DIVISION

Tom, the Vice President of the Product Development Division who had hired him, saw Frank and warmly greeted him. Sensing Frank's plight, Tom said he was sorry that Frank was held up by all of the first-day administrative details. He briefly introduced Frank to some of the other department managers, and then led Frank to his new office. Tom said there was some information on the desk that Frank should look at. He told Frank that he had to go to another meeting, but that Ann, in the office next door, could help him if he had any questions.

Frank had been rushing around all day, and needed a few moments to himself. He went exploring down the hallway and found the rest room. Upon entering his office, Frank surveyed it in detail. It was spacious and had a nice view through a floor-to-ceiling window. He saw a top-of-the-line computer in one corner, and a small table with chairs in the other. As he sat down behind his desk, the left side of the chair sank about two inches. *"Oh well,"* he thought, *"when this office was vacant somebody probably exchanged this crippled chair for a better one. I'm sure I'll have a good chair by tomorrow."*

He shifted his focus to the two-foot high stack of manuals on the desk. He opened the first one and began browsing through it. Frank was a master at sizing up manuals, and within a few minutes he commented aloud, *"Boy, do they need help! The material is probably technically accurate, but I would rather use this manual to put myself to sleep than read it to figure out how to use the software it describes. It's poorly organized and written in an unfriendly style. It must leave customers feeling pretty cold and helpless."*

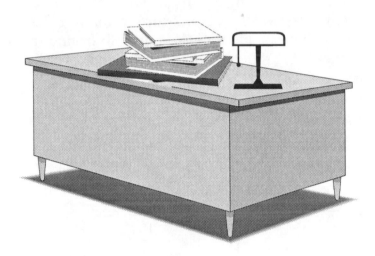

He also mused—this time silently, *"This is kind of like my experience today. Metasoft seems to do a good job at recruiting new customers and employees, but once somebody signs on, the communication just isn't there."* He began to wonder whether he had made a mistake by joining Metasoft.

The rest of the day, Frank skimmed through the stack of manuals and made some quick notes about what he saw as their failings and what he would like to see happen within the department under his direction. At 4:45 P.M. Frank received a call from Tom's secretary. Tom wanted to meet with Frank at 8:30 A.M. the next morning.

Frank looked forward to his meeting with Tom. He saw it as an opportunity to begin working toward his goals. Tom, unfortunately, had other priorities. He had proofs for a 10-page product brochure developed by the Marketing Department, and he needed someone to edit it. He thought this was Frank's forte, so he made proofreading the brochure his first assignment.

Frank left the meeting discouraged. During his career he had certainly put in his share of time proofreading, in fact his colleagues called him *"old eagle eyes."* But he expected to be doing something a little more challenging after 20 years!

Frank accomplished the proofreading task by 2 P.M. and to his delight, Ann asked him if he would like to join her and a group of people from their department for a late lunch. At lunch, Frank met several of the people he would be managing. They impressed him with their enthusiasm for his vision for the department.

Back at Metasoft, Frank continued the lunchtime conversation with Ann. She was one of the senior members of the department, and was willing to fill him in on what the department was doing. It was apparent that Ann would be Frank's best resource for finding out the information he needed and providing him with a clear, in-depth orientation to the Metasoft *"culture."*

During his first week, Frank met daily with Ann. She helped him get established, and introduced him to people inside and outside the department. She was always available to respond to his questions—from a simple *"How do I log on to the computer network?"* to something as elaborate as *"What is the status of every project we're working on in this department?"*

By the end of his second week, Frank felt comfortable in his work situation, and he had developed a preliminary year long plan of action to present to Tom. In his third week, Frank and Tom met, and together they hammered out a detailed plan for expanding Frank's department and upgrading its products over the next year.

Frank and Tom agreed to meet weekly to review Frank's progress in achieving the plan. At the end of the first month, Frank was right on schedule. There were rumors, however, that the organization would undergo budget cuts. Over the next few months, the rumors proved to be true, and Frank and Tom had to modify the year long plan to account for a 10 percent budget cut.

By the end of his first year at Metasoft, Frank was one of the organization's most successful managers. Others saw his department as a cohesive team focused on its mission of creating state-of-the-art product reference and training materials.

Fortunately, Frank's rocky start during his first days at Metasoft didn't cast a lasting cloud over his employment. The events of the first few days did, however, cause him considerable concern that could have been easily prevented. This guidebook will show what you *(and Frank)* can do to prevent the new employees you hire from experiencing similar orientation disappointments and discouragements.

CHAPTER TWO WORKSHEET:
LEARNING FROM EXPERIENCE

1. What made Frank's first day a bad experience?

_____

_____

_____

_____

2. What impressions do you think Frank formed about Metasoft as a result of his *"orientation."*

_____

_____

_____

_____

_____

_____

_____

_____

3. What are some of the possible consequences of a poor orientation?

_____

_____

_____

_____

_____

_____

_____

_____

_____

_____

_____

_____

_____

_____

_____

_____

THE NEED FOR A PLAN

A Test To Rate Job Orientation

Think back to the last chapter about Frank James' experience when he first started his new job at Metasoft. How would you rate his orientation? Review each statement below and indicate either T *(true)* or F *(false)*. Add up the number of T's and F's, then look at the scoring key to see how Frank fared.

TRUE or FALSE

T or F

_____ 1. Frank felt welcome.

_____ 2. It appeared that the appropriate people were expecting Frank.

_____ 3. Frank was given an opportunity to ask questions or otherwise participate in the orientation process.

_____ 4. Frank didn't spend a lot of time waiting for others *(due to their busy schedules)*.

_____ 5. Frank's boss made time to meet with him and make him feel comfortable.

_____ 6. Frank's orientation seemed well planned.

_____ 7. Frank was informed about the organization's culture *(environment)*.

_____ 8. Organizational policies (*e.g., pay, benefits, etc.*) were clearly explained to Frank.

_____ 9. Frank learned about the organization's history.

_____ 10. The organization's future plans were explained to Frank.

_____ 11. Frank was introduced to the organization's products/services.

_____ 12. Frank understood the organization's philosophy and expectations of its employees.

_____ 13. Frank's office area was set up and ready for him.

_____ 14. Frank was introduced to his coworkers.

_____ 15. Frank received a copy of his job description and an explanation of his role.

_____ 16. Frank was given a tour of the facility.

_____ 17. Frank was given a work assignment, rather than just an opportunity to "*read*" manuals.

_____ 18. The organizational chart was explained to Frank and he understood where his job fit in.

_____ 19. Frank went to lunch on his first day with his supervisor.

_____ 20. At the end of his first week, Frank felt like a "*team member.*"

TOTAL: _____ TRUE _____ FALSE

SCORING KEY

18 – 20 True   Frank was very lucky to receive such a thorough and well-planned orientation. Metasoft should keep up the program.

✦ ✦ ✦

15 – 17 True   Frank's orientation was better than what most people receive. However, his orientation could have been more effective.

✦ ✦ ✦

11 – 14 True   Unfortunately, Frank received an orientation that is pretty typical for most organizations. Metasoft should improve its overall orientation process.

✦ ✦ ✦

10 or less True   Congratulations to Frank for sticking it out! Metasoft should start over and create a new orientation process.

Your scoring probably indicated that you think Frank received a rather poor orientation to his new job. Frank's experience certainly isn't unique—in fact, you may have had a similar experience yourself!

The Importance Of An Orientation Plan

The problem in Frank's case *(and perhaps in yours)* was a lack of a meaningful job orientation plan. What transpired during his first critical day, week, and month simply happened. There was little intervention from anyone to make sure that Frank's orientation was effective because there was no thought-out, written-down, detailed orientation plan.

Unfortunately, when there is no plan, supervisors tend to imitate the orientation process they underwent when they first began at the organization, regardless of whether or not it was effective. Important things that everyone working at an organization takes for granted—such as the location of the rest room and when to go to lunch—are often overlooked!

PLAN OF ACTION

WHAT	WHO	WHEN	TIME	DONE
~ ~ ~ ~	~ ~	~ ~	~ ~	✓
~ ~ ~ ~	~ ~	~ ~	~ ~	✓
~ ~ ~ ~	~ ~	~ ~	~ ~	✓
~ ~ ~ ~	~ ~	~ ~	~ ~	✓

An orientation plan ensures that you cover everything and nothing is left to chance. As a manager or supervisor, you don't need to develop and implement an orientation plan for your new employees by yourself. You can work it out in concert with the new employee, others in your department, and your organization's Human Resources Department. You can rely on other employees to help carry it out, especially the new employee.

Your job as a manager or supervisor is to integrate new employees effectively into your department or work group. The chapters that follow lead you step-by-step through the process of developing and implementing an effective on-the-job orientation and training plan.

CHAPTER THREE WORKSHEET:
NEW EMPLOYEE ORIENTATION CHECKLIST

_____   _____

New Employee's Name   **Start Date**

During the first three months of employment, the new employee's hiring supervisor and/or designated department representative should cover the following items :

Check If Done:

_____ **1.** Provide essential resources and references:

     ____ Organizational marketing literature   ____ Organizational charts
     ____ Product/service promotions, etc.   ____ Job descriptions
     ____ Mission, values, philosophy, etc.   ____ HR/policy manual
     ____ Strategic plans, goals, objectives, etc.   ____ Employee handbook
     ____ Organizational and departmental procedures   ____ Key forms, checklists, etc.

_____ **2.** Review the job description and performance expectations/standards

_____ **3.** Review the work schedule (include lunch, breaks, overtime, time clock, etc.)

_____ **4.** Review the payroll timing, policies, and procedures

_____ **5.** Review key policies:

     ____ Attendance/punctuality   ____ Personal conduct standards
     ____ Sick days/leaves of absence   ____ Progressive disciplinary actions
       (e.g., who to notify)   ____ Confidentiality
     ____ Holidays   ____ Safety/accident procedures
     ____ Vacations/scheduling procedures   ____ Health/first aid
     ____ Standard work shift   ____ Emergency procedures
     ____ Overtime   ____ Preventive maintenance
     ____ Performance appraisal   ____ Conflict of interest
     ____ Wage/salary administration   ____ Smoking/nonsmoking areas
     ____ Dress code   ____ Visitors
     ____ Office appearance   ____ Personal status changes

_____ **6.** Review general administrative procedures:

     ____ Time cards   ____ Business cards
     ____ Office/desk/work station keys   ____ ID cards/security access
     ____ Calendars/schedules   ____ Expense reports
     ____ Pertinent reports/lists   ____ General supplies

_____ **7.** Give introductions to members of immediate staff (include brief background of each) and other key personnel

_____ **8.** Review standard meetings to attend:

MEETINGS	PURPOSE	MEMBERS	TIMES
a.			
b.			
c.			

_____ **9.** Give a brief tour of the surrounding area and facilities, including:

____ Rest rooms	____ Equipment/tools/supplies
____ Telephones/message systems	____ Storage/files
____ Pay phones	____ Books/references
____ Mail distribution/center	____ Break room/kitchen
____ Copy machines/fax	____ Coffee/vending machines
____ Bulletin boards	____ Eating establishments
____ Appointment books/schedules	____ Drinking fountains
____ Time clock	____ Parking
____ Computer systems/printers	____ Emergency exits

_____ **10.** Present initial job assignments and training plans.

ASSIGNMENTS	TRAINING PLANS
a.	
b.	
c.	
d.	

_____ **11.** Identify coworkers (*other than the hiring supervisor*) who will train the new employee and/or act as a "buddy" to assist with general questions:

GO TO THIS COWORKER	FOR TRAINING AND/OR ASSISTANCE REGARDING
a.	
b.	

_____ **12.** Plan for initial lunches (*designate someone to spend time with the new employee, such as a member of the management team, coworkers, and/or other employees during the first few days/weeks*)

_____ **13.** Other: _____

_____ _____ _____ _____
Hiring Supervisor's Signature   Date   New Employee's Signature   Date

CRITICAL LEAD-UP TO DAY ONE

A Sharing Of Responsibilities And Roles

In your day-to-day activities as a manager or supervisor, you have enough to do without having to take full responsibility for an employee orientation plan. The burden of devising and carrying out such a plan can and should be shared between the Human Resources Department and the new employee's department.

Although the specific roles and responsibilities of the Human Resources Department vary with the size and distinctive characteristics of an organization, one of its important missions is to provide a general organizational orientation program for new employees.

As a department manager or supervisor, you have your own unique responsibilities in employee orientation. After all, the employees that come into your department will be reporting to you. Thus, you must make sure that they are quickly and effectively assimilated into your organization as productive team members.

In fact, most employees feel that the departmental orientation is more important than the organizational orientation typically conducted by Human Resources Departments. Unfortunately, many organizations focus much more time and energy on the overall orientation. The key to an effective orientation process is the development and implementation of a coordinated plan.

The Human Resources Department generally assumes responsibility for introducing new employees to the organization. The Human Resources Department may have a general orientation program already in place, and in carrying out that program it may assume responsibility for activities such as:

⇨ Planning the specific content of the overall organizational orientation

⇨ Scheduling orientation speakers

⇨ Preparing orientation media and materials

⇨ Reserving space for an orientation meeting

⇨ Scheduling employees

⇨ Making opening and closing remarks

⇨ Introducing orientation speakers

⇨ Conducting facility tours

⇨ Evaluating and refining the general orientation program

Even if the Human Resources Department has a good orientation program, most of what a new employee needs will not be provided. New employees need specific information and help from you, their manager or supervisor. Your responsibilities in orienting new employees to your department include:

DEPARTMENT MANAGER RESPONSIBILITIES

⟹ Providing a positive role model
⟹ Providing specific information about the department and the job
⟹ Coordinating all orientation activities after the general orientation
⟹ Introducing new employees to the organization
⟹ Being available and accessible
⟹ Ensuring the new employee has the tools and resources to be successful
⟹ Evaluating and refining your department's orientation plan

New employee orientation will only be effective when the Human Resources Department and department managers or supervisors share responsibilities and coordinate their specific roles.

The Organization's "Orientation Survival Kit"

New employees need a variety of information that will help them understand the following:

Ⅎ Organizational standards, expectations, and norms

Ⅎ Traditions and policies

Ⅎ Desired social behaviors

Ⅎ Technical aspects of the job

One way to address these needs is to provide each employee with an *"Orientation Survival Kit."* Your Human Resources Department should already have these kits prepared. If they don't, you *(or the department secretary)* can develop one for future employees. Make sure to keep all material together in one folder, such as a three-ring binder, and include critical survival information.

ORIENTATION SURVIVAL KIT

- A *current organizational chart*
- A *projected organizational chart*
- Map of the facility
- Key terms and acronyms unique to the industry, organization, and/or job
- Copy of policy handbook(s) (*e.g., covering expense report process*)
- Copy of union contract(s)
- Copy of specific job goals and description
- List of observed holidays
- List of fringe benefits
- Copies of performance evaluation forms, dates, and procedures
- Copies of other required forms (*e.g., supply requisition and expense reimbursement*)
- List of on-the-job training opportunities
- Sources of information (*e.g., organizational/departmental libraries, computer databases*)
- Detailed outline of emergency and accident prevention procedures
- Sample copy of each important publication for the organization
- Telephone numbers and locations of key personnel and operations
- Copies of insurance plans
- Other information to "*survive*" the first weeks and months

Your Departmental Orientation Checklist

In addition to the information contained in an *"Orientation Survival Kit,"* new employees also need specific information about the department they are joining. Here's a checklist, organized by category, that you can use to determine what you need to convey to new employees. Within each category, identify those items relevant to your department.

Think about what items you need to address during a new employee's first day. Also consider which items to cover within the first week, month, six months, and year of employment. You will use this information to develop a new employee orientation and training plan for your department.

Employee Orientation!

1st Week - 1st Month
6 Months - 1st Year

ORIENTATION CHECKLIST

Departmental functions

✓ Goals and current priorities

✓ Organization and structure

✓ Operational activities

✓ Relationship of functions to other departments

✓ Relationships of jobs within the department

Job duties and responsibilities

✓ Detailed explanation of job based on current job description and expected results

✓ Explanation of why the job is important, how the specific job relates to others in the department and organization

✓ Discussion of common problems and how to avoid and overcome them

✓ Performance standards and basis of performance evaluation

✓ Number of daily work hours and times

✓ Overtime needs and requirements

✓ Extra duty assignments (*e.g., changing duties to cover for an absent worker*)

✓ Required records and reports

✓ Check-out of equipment to be used

✓ Explanation of where and how to get tools, how equipment is maintained, and repaire procedures

✓ Types of assistance available, when and how to ask for help

✓ Relations with state and federal inspectors

Policies, procedures, rules, and regulations

✓ Rules unique to the job and/or department

✓ Handling emergencies

✓ Safety precautions and accident prevention

✓ Reporting of hazards and accidents

✓ Security, theft problems, and costs

✓ Cleanliness standards and sanitation (*e.g., clean-up*)

✓ Relations with outside people (*e.g., drivers*)

✓ Eating, smoking, and chewing gum, etc., in department area

✓ Removal of things from department

✓ Damage control (*e.g., smoking restrictions*)

✓ Time clock and time sheets

✓ Breaks and rest periods

✓ Lunch duration and time

✓ Making and receiving personal telephone calls

✓ Requisitioning supplies and equipment

✓ Monitoring and evaluating employee performance

✓ Job bidding and requesting reassignment

✓ Going to cars during work hours

Tour of department

✓ Rest rooms and showers

✓ Fire alarm box and fire extinguisher stations

✓ Time clocks

✓ Lockers

✓ Approved entrances and exits

✓ Water fountains and eye-wash systems

✓ Supervisor's and work group's work space

✓ Supply room and maintenance department

✓ Sanitation and security offices

✓ Smoking areas

✓ Locations of services to employees related to department

✓ First aid kit

New Employee Orientation

Key Questions To Ask When Planning An Employee's First Day

No one has as much influence on a new employee as you do as a manager or supervisor. You can sharpen the plan for the new employee's first day by asking yourself the following questions:

1. What things would the new employee need to know about this new environment that would make her comfortable? List all the possibilities you can think of.

2. What impressions should the new employee have on the first day? Don't worry about the *"how to"* at the moment—focus on the *"what."*

3. What key policies and procedures must you make the employee aware of on the first day so that mistakes won't be made on the second day? Don't plan too far ahead, and stick only to vital issues.

4. What specific things can you do to ensure that the new employee will begin to know her fellow employees without feeling overwhelmed? List as many as practical for the first day.

5. What special things—such as providing the new employee with her own desk or work area— can you do to make her feel physically comfortable, welcome, and secure?

6. What job-related tasks can you reasonably teach the new employee to do well that first day to provide her with a sense of accomplishment? List no more than three things, and one may be sufficient.

7. What positive experience can you provide for the new employee to talk about to the *"folks at home"*? This item should relate to something that could make her feel valued in the job situation.

8. How can you be available on the new employee's first day to ensure personal attention, and to convey a clear message that she is an important addition to the work team?

IMPORTANT ADDITION!

Frank's Meeting With The Human Resources Department

To clarify their respective responsibilities and roles, Frank arranged a meeting between himself and the key people in the Human Resources Department. Frank spoke first at the meeting. In an alarmingly direct manner that he had become famous for, he bluntly said, *"We have a problem. My first day at Metasoft was an insult and a disaster, and I'm afraid we're continuing to inflict similar pain and suffering on our new employees. When I arrived at Metasoft, nobody here knew I was starting. Once you figured that out, you threw a mountain of paperwork at me and then shuffled me off to some health clinic for more paperwork and a physical exam."*

"Once I got through all that, the people in the Product Development Division treated me no better. They scheduled me to go to a meeting that I missed through no fault of my own. I met them as they were leaving the meeting, and they were at least kind enough to escort me to my office. Then they abandoned me so that I could spend the rest of the day acquainting myself with a stack of boring manuals. I ended my first day here feeling overwhelmed with paperwork, ignored, and altogether negative about my new job and the organization!"

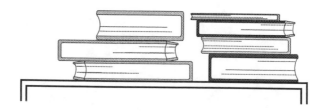

"Recently I've spent a lot of time recruiting top-notch people for my department. When they start their new jobs here, I don't want them to go through what I went through. We must come up with a better way to orient new employees! In this meeting we need to define our various roles and responsibilities, and figure out how to accomplish an effective and coordinated employee orientation."

The Human Resources people were initially taken aback by Frank's outspokenness. But as they discussed his points further, they realized the need for improvement. They agreed to use a flip chart to define Human Resources'and the hiring department's responsibilities. It seemed to them that the Human Resources Department's responsibilities centered on personnel and administrative issues. They specifically agreed to take responsibility for:

➡ Helping new employees complete the necessary employment paperwork

➡ Providing an Orientation Survival Kit to all new employees

➡ Explaining the company's benefits, policies, and general procedures

Frank questioned why it was necessary for every new employee to have a physical exam at the health clinic on the first day of work. Since most people start a new job on Monday, he thought it made more sense to go for the physical on Tuesday. The health clinic would be less busy then, and this change of procedure would allow new employees to experience less stress on their first day. Everyone agreed this was a good suggestion, and that they could easily implement it.

For his part, Frank concluded that he needed to take responsibility for the following:

⇨ Making sure each new employee has an office and the appropriate equipment and supplies

⇨ Coordinating with the Human Resources Department to ensure smooth scheduling for orientation activities

⇨ Greeting each new employee

⇨ Introducing each new employee to the appropriate people in the department

⇨ Providing each new employee with a tour of the departmental and organizational facilities

⇨ Checking how a new employee's first day went and answering any end-of-the-day questions

⇨ Creating a customized orientation and training plan for each new employee

⇨ Periodically monitoring and adjusting the orientation and training plan for each new employee

CHAPTER FOUR WORKSHEET:
ACTION PLAN FOR COORDINATION

Schedule a meeting with the Human Resources Department to determine:

➡ The role of Human Resources in the orientation program

➡ The role of the hiring manager

➡ How the organizational and departmental orientations will be coordinated and integrated

❏ If you do not have a Human Resources Department that handles new employee orientation, make sure your orientation plan includes these *"general organizational"* orientation items.

❏ Contact key employees who may have an interest in helping with department orientation. Share your *"vision"* of a good orientation and how they fit into that vision.

❏ Provide rewards and recognition to employees who participate in the orientation process.

❏ Assemble an *"Orientation Survival Kit"* to be used as a *"model"* for the entire company (*e.g., department administrative personnel*) when constructing a *"kit"* for new employees.

❏ Develop a process for constantly updating the orientation checklist to ensure it is continuously improved. One approach may be to ask each new employee to review the checklist and make suggestions on how to improve the list.

❏ Review key questions on pages 38 and 39 in a staff meeting and record the answers for use with the next new employee hired.

CHAPTER FIVE

DAY ONE: SURVIVAL

An employee's first day on the job can be a very disappointing, even frightening experience—as Frank James can attest to. For most new employees, the first day is a matter of finding themselves in a totally unfamiliar environment, surrounded by people they don't know. All the things a new employee took for granted at his or her old job—including the camaraderie of coworkers, where everything is located, and how to use the phone and other equipment—are now suddenly gone and replaced by a new, strange workplace.

In your role as a manager or supervisor, however, you can do three things to alleviate a new employee's first-day apprehension:

> ☞ Introduce the new employee to people they will be contacting and dealing with on a regular basis
>
> ☞ Take care of the logistical concerns of the new employee (*e.g., location of the restroom, cafeteria, etc.*)
>
> ☞ End the employee's first day with a personal wrap-up to answer questions and reassure the employee

May I Present . . .

When a new employee reports to work for the first time, devote several minutes to putting him at ease and establishing a positive rapport. Personally describe the scheduled activities of the day to him. If you have a great deal planned for the day, be sure to provide the new employee with a typed agenda so that he doesn't have to remember everything or need to take notes.

After going over the day's activities, introduce the new worker to others with whom he will be working. Generally, these people will all be in the same department, but your introductions may extend to people in other groups. If there are more than five or six introductions, it's a good idea to have a sheet typed in advance listing everyone's name, title, office location, and telephone extension. It might be helpful to include an organizational chart showing employees and their extension numbers.

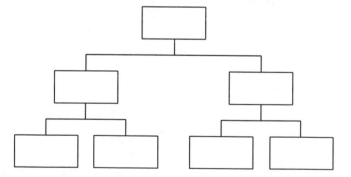

Where Am I?

Once you introduce the new employee, it's time to show him exactly where he will be working, and to explain where everything is located.

Generally, you don't need to show the new employee around yourself; you can assign a sponsor for this purpose. The person you select as the new employee's sponsor should be thoroughly familiar with the layout of the area and the new employee's job function. The sponsor should also be able to devote as much time as needed to answer logistical questions, and to provide the new employee with work manuals, instructions, or any other printed materials relevant to their job.

Your sponsor should include the following key activities (*where applicable*) during the course of the logistical orientation:

1. Show the new employee his office, desk, or work area.

2. Show the employee where supplies are located and how to order them.

3. Provide the employee with a telephone directory, and explain how the phone system works.

4. Show the employee the location of rest rooms and water fountains.

5. Show the employee how to operate the photocopy and fax machines, or any other equipment he will use.

6. Show the employee the location of files, manuals, and other reference material.

7. Introduce the employee to the food service facilities inside and outside of the organization.

8. Show the employee the lounge.

9. Show the employee the exercise facilities.

10. Explain the procedure for medical care.

11. Show the employee the child-care facilities.

It's a good idea to give the new employee a list highlighting the key activities, so that he can make notes. Some of the points mentioned––such as the cafeteria, employee lounge, exercise facility, and child-care facility––may also be included in a tour conducted as part of the organizational orientation provided by the Human Resources Department. Even if this is the case, repetition can only serve to reinforce what the employee is being shown.

By the time the lunch hour approaches on an employee's first day, he is probably feeling somewhat overwhelmed. Therefore, arrangements should be made for someone to take the new person to lunch. This may be done by you or the sponsor in charge of showing the new employee around. Sometimes a new employee's coworkers can assume this responsibility. In any event, the new employee should have lunch with someone who they can rely on to help them get situated.

If your organization has a cafeteria, it's a good idea to have lunch there so that the new employee can become familiar with it. In addition, the cafeteria provides an excellent opportunity for the new employee to be informally introduced to other employees. Alternatively, if your organization has an executive dining room and the new employee is eligible to eat there, you may want to plan on having lunch there the first day.

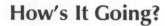

How's It Going?

Regardless of how the new employee's first day is spent, it should conclude the way it began: with a meeting between the employee and you. Set aside approximately half an hour to discuss what took place during the day, as well as to answer any questions the new employee may have. In addition to this end-of-day wrap-up, briefly review the agenda for the next day so that the new employee has something specific to anticipate.

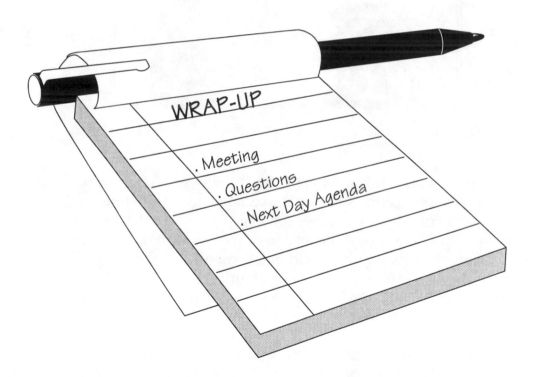

Back to Frank . . .

It had only been a few weeks since Frank had his meeting with the Human Resources Department. He felt it ended on a positive note, with both parties having a clear understanding of each other's orientation roles and responsibilities. Janet, a recent hire, was scheduled to start the following Monday, and Frank was anxious to implement his orientation strategy with her.

Janet was an interactive multimedia specialist with an extensive background in both the software and healthcare industries. Frank wanted to ensure that during her first day she would feel graciously welcomed. On the Friday before she started, Frank contacted the Human Resources Department to make sure they knew Janet was arriving Monday.

He briefly went over what they discussed in their meeting, and verified that they would have everything ready for her at the designated time. He also made sure that Janet's office was in order, and that Bruce Jenkins (*from his department*) was available Monday to spend time with Janet. Finally, he told the receptionist in the lobby to watch for Janet's arrival Monday morning.

Human Resources Please!

Janet arrived in the Metasoft lobby at exactly 8 A.M. the following Monday. The receptionist told her that Frank was expecting her and that he would be out shortly. A moment later, Frank came into the lobby smiling brightly. He cordially greeted Janet, offered her coffee, and then took her back to his office. They exchanged pleasantries for awhile, and then Frank expressed how glad he was that Janet was joining the department.

Then Frank said, *"Janet, after we finish talking, I'll take you around the department to meet everyone. Then I'm going to turn you over to Bruce Jenkins, one of our senior writers. He'll show you your office, tell you where everything is, and explain how to get around. Feel free to ask Bruce a lot of questions—he knows the ropes as well as anyone in the department. I'll meet you back here at 11:45 A.M. so that we can go to lunch. I've made reservations for us at the Park Avenue Grill down the street; the food there is excellent and the atmosphere is relaxing.*

After lunch at 1 P.M., Bruce will take you over to the Human Resources Department to fill out the necessary employment paperwork. While you're there, Candice will give you an Orientation Survival Kit and explain the organization's benefits, general policies, and procedures. When that ends at about 4:45 P.M., come back to my office so that we can talk. I'll answer any questions you may have formed throughout the day, and we can also discuss tomorrow's schedule."

CHAPTER FOUR WORKSHEET:
EVALUATING YOUR DAY ONE ACTIVITIES

Based on what you have read so far, answer the following questions about your organizational and departmental orientations:

1. How would you rate the effectiveness of the first-day orientation experience for most new employees in your department?

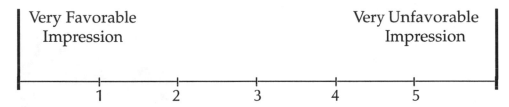

Very Favorable Impression				Very Unfavorable Impression
1	2	3	4	5

2. Explain your rating:

_____

_____

3. What are three specific things you can do to improve the first-day orientation process?

_____

_____

4. What are three specific things others can do to improve the first-day orientation process?

_____

_____

CHAPTER SIX

WEEK ONE: COMING UP FOR AIR

Once an employee successfully ends his first day, your responsibility for providing job orientation isn't over—in fact, it's just begun. Early in the employee's first week, you will need to devise a specific orientation plan for her. This orientation plan is one that you work out directly with the employee to meet her individual needs.

Key Questions For The First Week

To help you devise an effective, individualized orientation plan for a new employee, first review your departmental orientation checklist. This checklist, which was described in Chapter Four, includes general orientation items for any new employee in your department. As you're reviewing your departmental orientation checklist, ask yourself the following questions:

1. What does this new employee need to know by the end of the first week? Develop your list, sequence the items, and then schedule them. Also ask yourself what experiences from this employee's first day need reinforcement. Recall the wrap-up with the employee at the end of the first day and think about what the employee may not have absorbed or had concerns about.

2. What key policies and procedures do you need to convey to this employee during the first week? Those items most critical to the employee's job success are best handled now. Because the new employee will probably regard the policies and procedures you communicate in the first five days as *"the rule,"* be sure to go over the critical ones.

3. What positive behaviors do you want to reinforce during this employee's first week? By keeping the answer to this question clearly before you, you will avoid negative behaviors later on.

4. What should you do to help integrate this new employee into a particular work group and the department as a whole? By the end of the first week, social relationships will have begun to develop. For better or worse, the new employee will end the week having a fairly good idea of how the other employees regard her. List what you can do to ensure that the new employee doesn't feel *"left out."*

5. How can you give this new employee a sense of accomplishment during the first week? Nearly every job, except perhaps the most complex ones, should offer a solid emotional payoff by the end of the first week. List specific work assignments that offer a rewarding experience for the employee.

6. What feedback will this new employee need? It's important for you to get together with the employee periodically to talk about progress and problems. At this point, your main concern is deciding what the new employee needs feedback on and how much feedback is appropriate.

7. How can you make yourself accessible to this new employee? Effectively managing your time is always tough, but be aware that the hours you invest in the first week with the new employee may save you hundreds of hours in the weeks and years to come. Assess what you need to do with the new employee, estimate how long it will take, schedule the activity, and then commit yourself to carrying out your schedule.

The Orientation Plan

Your answers to the seven key questions tell you what needs to be included in the individualized orientation plan for a new employee. But you also need to determine who is responsible for each item, the order in which they will occur, and how much time each item will take to complete.

Work out the specifics of the orientation plan by meeting with the new employee. During this meeting, come to a mutual agreement about what activities to include in the plan and how to schedule them. The employee should feel ownership of the orientation plan and the greatest responsibility in carrying it out.

The simplest way to create an orientation plan is to fill out a chart with these headings:

WHAT	BY WHOM	BY WHEN	TIME	DONE

Under the *"What"* column enter the activities that you and the employee agreed to include in the orientation plan. The *"By Whom"* column simply identifies the person or persons responsible for a task, while the *"By When"* column indicates the deadline for accomplishing it. The *"Time"* column indicates the amount of time you estimate for completing the item. The *"Done"* column is for checking off a completed item.

Week In Review

At the end of the employee's first week you should have a review meeting. This meeting serves two important purposes:

1. It enables you and the employee to review the orientation plan and check off the *"done"* items. This process visibly confirms the employee's accomplishments and progress.

2. It makes you aware of how the plan may need to be adjusted. For example, upon attempting to accomplish one of the items on the plan, the employee may discover that she needs additional information or training. These discoveries are helpful in revising the plan to make it more effective.

Janet's First Week

Based on his brief meeting with Janet at the end of her first day, Frank concluded that she still needed to gain an understanding of the department's goals, as well as her specific role as a multimedia specialist. He also wanted to identify areas in which Janet felt she lacked information or needed training. In addition, he wanted to come up with a significant assignment that Janet could complete during the first week.

Thus, Frank met with Janet the next day to work out a detailed orientation plan.

During their hour-long meeting, Frank and Janet came up with this orientation plan for her first week:

WHAT	BY WHOM	BY WHEN	TIME	DONE
Go over departmental and organizational charts and identify Janet's role	Frank Janet	1/26	1 hour	
Get user account set up on computer network	Janet, Bill	1/27	1 hour	
Learn how to use E-mail system	Janet, Bill	1/27	2 hours	
Attend customer training course for medical billing product	Janet	1/27 1/28 1/29	15 hours	
Review and evaluate on-line help for medical billing product	Janet	1/27 1/28 1/29 1/30	15 hours	
Attend departmental staff meeting	Janet	1/30	1 hour	

At the end of Janet's first week, Frank and Janet met again. They went over Janet's orientation plan, checking off each item she completed. Her review of their on-line help for the medical billing product showed it could be substantially improved with little effort. However, she asked Frank if she could learn more about the Windows Help Engine (WHE), a computer application Metasoft used to create the medical billing product. Frank agreed, and they added WHE training to Janet's orientation plan.

MONTH ONE: LOOKING AROUND

View a new employee's orientation and training as a continuous process rather than as a single event. The orientation and training you do at the departmental level may take a month, six months, or even a full year to complete! Your task in orienting and training a new employee is to provide all the information and tools they need to work effectively and productively.

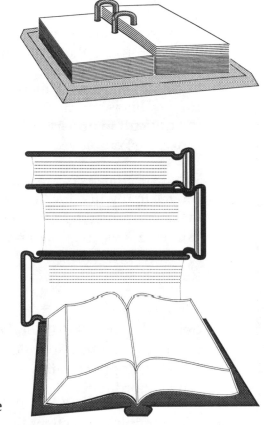

Key Questions For The First Month

During the first month, provide the new employee with additional details about his role in his immediate work group, department, and organization. In addition, be sure to provide the new employee with more information about his specific job. The following list of questions will help you clarify what should go into the evolving orientation plan for a new employee.

ORIENTATION QUESTIONS

1. What additional things does the new employee need to know by the end of the first month? Review your earlier lists for items that might extend into a long-term process.

2. What policies and procedures could affect the new employee's job performance? If your organization has a policy and procedures manual, check the index to ensure that you consider everything.

3. What impressions or models do you want to reinforce? This is a particularly challenging area because it's difficult to impart organizational values to an individual employee.

4. What specific tasks can you assign to the new employee that will allow for growth? Examine all the tasks performed by members of the employee's immediate work group and structure the simpler ones into interesting and challenging assignments for the new employee.

5. What can your organization do to broaden its delegation of authority and decision making? Concentrate on getting specific tasks done, and then search for opportunities to share your own tasks with subordinates.

6. What training objectives do you want to meet within the employee's first month?

Monitoring And Adjusting The Orientation Plan

The orientation plan you work out with a new employee during his first week isn't static—it should reflect a dynamic ongoing process. It includes both short- and long-term activities, and you must constantly monitor and update it to meet your objectives and the employee's needs.

An essential part of monitoring a new employee's orientation plan is meeting regularly with him. During these meetings, which may occur weekly or less frequently, obtain feedback from the employee about his progress in working through the plan. These meetings will also give you an opportunity to express your thoughts on the employee's progress.

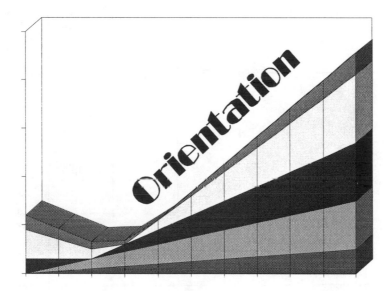

As you and the employee review the orientation plan, you may discover that it's desirable to make some adjustments to it. These adjustments may include adding and removing items as well as resequencing some items to accommodate changes in the employee's assignments or your specific objectives.

Janet's First Month

During the first month of Janet's employment, Frank met with her weekly. Their meetings focused on monitoring and adjusting Janet's evolving orientation plan, as well as how she could take increasing responsibility for fulfilling her role as a multimedia specialist in the Product Documentation Department.

March

					Frank	
					Frank	
					Frank	
					Frank	
					Frank	

Frank gave Janet her first long-term assignment: to develop a preliminary design for an on-line, interactive Help system for Metasoft's medical billing product. This assignment was an important part of Frank's overall plan to create state-of-the-art product reference and training materials. He also felt it would be a challenging task for Janet; one that would enable her to acquire pertinent information and tools. Frank wanted Janet to think about how she would accomplish this assignment, and he expected to add new items to her orientation plan in subsequent meetings.

What	By Whom	By When	Time	Done
Develop a preliminary design for an on-line Help system	Janet	2/31	80 hours	

CHAPTER SEVEN WORKSHEET: REVIEW OF QUESTIONS

A. Review the questions that were discussed on page 64. Answer those questions below for your new employee.

1.

_____

_____

_____

2.

_____

_____

_____

3.

_____

_____

_____

4.

_____

_____

_____

_____

5.

_____

_____

_____

6.

_____

_____

_____

B. Based on your answers, do you need to make changes in your orientation checklist or "*standard*" orientation plan?

_____

_____

SIX MONTHS: GETTING THERE

Within the first six months a new employee should become integrated into your organization and get *"up to speed"* in her job. As the new employee begins to have enough information to ask the *"right"* questions, she will then need more detailed explanations of the inner workings of your department and the organization at large. The new employee may also need more extensive training for this job.

Key Questions For The First Six Months

The following questions can help you define the orientation and training needs of a new employee during the first six-month period:

1. What additional things does the new employee need to know by the end of the first six months? Look over your department orientation checklist for relevant items not previously covered. For example, the new employee may need to know about safeguarding confidential information.

2. What additional policies and procedures does the new employee need to understand? These policies and procedures might include how your department relates to other departments or the next higher organizational level. It could also include the organization's policies regarding business travel and expenses.

3. What can you do to reduce the time needed to manage the new employee? There may be learning experiences, such as working with a more experienced employee, that might help.

4. How can you broaden the new employee's assignments so that she is continually challenged? The employee will experience growth in performing her job, and you need to match that growth with broader assignments.

5. What feedback should you give on the new employee's performance? If you meet regularly with the employee and monitor her progress on the orientation plan, you may already be providing some feedback on the employee's performance. You may also consider providing a performance evaluation at the end of the employee's first six months.

6. What training objectives do you want to meet within the employee's first six months?

Monitoring And Adjusting The Orientation Plan

You should continue meeting regularly with the new employee to monitor her progress. Although you may not need to meet as frequently as during the first month, the objectives should remain the same:

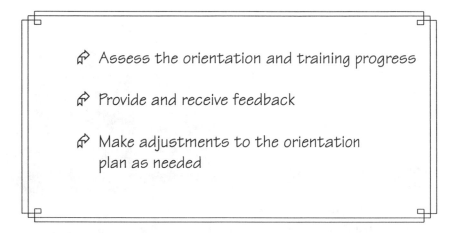

☞ Assess the orientation and training progress

☞ Provide and receive feedback

☞ Make adjustments to the orientation plan as needed

For example, as you monitor a new employee's progress, you may find the employee needs more detailed guidelines about how to deal with people at the corporate level. Your meetings with the employee are essential in discovering these needs and addressing them.

Janet's First Six Months

After the first month at Metasoft, Janet's main focus was designing a Help system for the medical billing product—the first major assignment Frank had given her. This assignment offered many challenges to Janet and gave her the opportunity to become more integrated into the department.

Frank continued to meet with Janet regularly. He listened to her concerns and offered suggestions. It soon became apparent to Frank that for Janet to do an effective job, she needed to develop a rapport with the Software Department. She also needed specific technical information about developing interactive systems in a multi-tasking environment. Both of these needs resulted in the following additions to her orientation and training plan:

WHAT	BY WHOM	BY WHEN	TIME	DONE
Meet with programming staff	Janet Bob Mary Mark	Each week	2 hours each week	
Attend conference on interaction	Janet	3/15-17	3 days	

CHAPTER EIGHT WORKSHEET: INTERVIEW GUIDE

1. Meet with employees inside and outside your department who have been with the organization for six to nine months. Ask them the following questions:

   A. What information did you need in the first six months that you did not receive?

   _____

   _____

   _____

   B. What tools and information were or would be helpful in the first six months?

   _____

   _____

   _____

   C. What changes would you make to the orientation process?

   _____

   _____

   _____

2. Based on the answers to the questions above, make changes to your orientation checklist or "*standard*" orientation plan.

CHAPTER NINE

TWELVE MONTHS: YOU'VE ARRIVED!

At the end of an employee's first year, everything should be coming together. He should be fully integrated as a productive member of your department. As the employee's first anniversary nears, look back to ensure that every aspect of the employee's orientation and training was adequately covered. Also review your overall department orientation checklist and plan to see how you can improve it.

1st Anniversary Congratulations!

Key Questions For The First Year

Keep in mind the following questions as you near the end of the employee's first year:

1. What additional things does this new employee need to know by the end of the first year? Review your departmental orientation checklist again to see if any relevant items have been omitted.

2. What additional policies and procedures does the new employee need to understand? If, for example, you've given the employee responsibility for supervising others or managing a project, he or she might require additional briefing.

3. How can you encourage the employee to be more self-sufficient? This concerns the gradual *"weaning"* of the new employee from dependence on others for help or information.

4. Does the employee have capabilities and skills that aren't being utilized? You may be able to give the employee new assignments or a change in job classification that would match his capabilities and skills better.

5. How well has the new employee met his goals? If the employee's performance isn't up to your expectations, try to understand why. The employee may have additional orientation and training needs that haven't been addressed.

6. What training objectives, if any, do you want to meet by the end of the employee's first year?

Monitoring And Adjusting The Orientation Plan

As you probably know by now, communication between you and a new employee is essential. Keep the lines of communication open by regularly meeting with the new employee and providing feedback on his progress. During these periodic meetings, monitor and adjust the employee's orientation plan, and evaluate his performance.

Janet's First Year

Frank continued meeting regularly with Janet during her first year. She had done a commendable job in designing an interactive on-line Help system. Through his observations and meetings with Janet, Frank realized that she had the makings of a first-rate project manager. She was skilled at problem solving, able to track progress at a detailed level, and good at motivating her fellow coworkers.

After about nine months with the organization, Frank decided with Janet's concurrence that she should expand her role as a multimedia specialist and take on some project management responsibilities. As a consequence, they modified her orientation and training plan to include the following items:

What	**By Whom**	**By When**	**Time**	**Done**
Learn how to use Metasoft's project management software	Janet Don	9/1	25 hours	
Attend company workshop for project managers	Janet	9/20-22	3 days	

ONGOING TRAINING: YOUR RESPONSIBILITY

Change is inevitable, especially in the workplace. Companies incorporate new technologies. They grow or, in some cases, downsize. They relocate, restructure, and merge. In addition, people in your department retire or leave, and new employees are hired.

The constancy of change in your organization and department means that you have an ongoing responsibility to communicate with the people you manage. You must continually inform them how each significant change impacts them. Fortunately, you have many opportunities to communicate effectively, including:

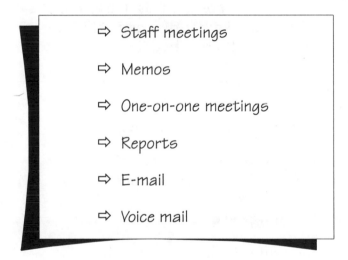

⇨ Staff meetings

⇨ Memos

⇨ One-on-one meetings

⇨ Reports

⇨ E-mail

⇨ Voice mail

Frank's Insight

After reflecting on his experiences as a new employee and as a manager, Frank realized that employee orientation and training never ends. It's a continuous cycle—much as the passage of one season into another—in the life of an organization and its workforce. There are always new goals to achieve, new technologies to utilize, new procedures to follow, and new people to include in the team.

Understanding The On-The-Job Training Process

Frank's insight led him to understand that he needed to have a defined process for ongoing training. After meeting with other managers, and discussing their issues with the Human Resources Department, Frank developed the following training process:

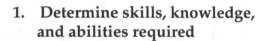

1. **Determine skills, knowledge, and abilities required**

    Identify the key responsibilities for the position. List the essential skills, knowledge, and abilities *(S/K/A's)* required for effective performance of each key responsibility.

2. **Assess present competency levels**

    Assess the present competency level of the employee for each responsibility and S/K/A.

3. **Identify training needs and objectives**

    Assess the relative importance of each responsibility and S/K/A to the employee's job using a scale such as 1 to 10 or 1 to 100. Assess the employee's competency level on the same scale. Then subtract your importance rating from your competency rating. The larger the negative number, the greater the need for training and improvement.

4. **Select behavioral outcomes, training methods, and training options**

   Include a list of what the employee will be able to do, conditions for attainment and standards, or criteria for acceptable performance.

5. **Finalize an on-the-job training plan**

   Include the desired behavioral outcome.

6. **Provide on-the-job training experiences**

   Use a *"hands-on"* approach with a qualified trainer; let the employee practice the task.

7. **Monitor training progress, resolve problems and control obstacles**

   Set up times to check back with the employee and observe her performance.

8. **Evaluate and reinforce progress toward training objectives and/or redirect and retrain**

   Look back at the criteria established; set up a method to rate the employee's performance on the task or skill.

Sample Training Needs/Objects Matrix

Frank asked Janet to apply the first three steps of this new process to Dana, the receptionist reassigned to Frank's department. Janet created the following form to identify training needs:

EMPLOYEE: Dana Mills	POSITION: Receptionist		DATE: 3/18
RESPONSIBILITY AND SKILLS/KNOWLEDGE/ABILITIES	**COMPETENCY RATING**	**IMPORTANCE RATING**	**TRAINING NEEDS**
1. Answer phones—			
a. pleasant, calm, clear and professional voice	5	5	0
b. legible writing skills for clear complete messages	2	4	-2
c. understand telephone system/technology	3	4	-1
2. Manage visitors—			
a. professional bearing, positive first impression	5	5	0
b. active listening skills to screen and assist visitors	4	4	0
c. knowledge of organization directory, people's roles	2	4	-2
3. Handle admin. duties—			
a. organizational skill to maintain phone directory	2	4	-2
b. diplomacy and detail to schedule conference rooms	5	2	+3

COMPETENCY RATING SCALE: 0 to 5; 0 = no experience and 5 = outstanding

IMPORTANCE RATING SCALE: 0 to 5; 0 = no importance and 5 = most importance

TRAINING NEEDS SCALE: In each row, subtract number in *"Importance Rating"* from the number in *"Competency Rating,"* (*please indicate a positive or negative number with a +/- sign*)

Clarifying Training Needs And Objectives

Effective on-the-job training objectives typically satisfy the following broad characteristics:

> ⇒ Identify the skills, abilities, knowledge and/or attitudes which are the desired outcomes of training
>
> ⇒ Are written clearly, using precise action-oriented words
>
> ⇒ Describe changes in behavior and/or performance desired as an outcome of training

To maximize the usefulness of skill-oriented, on-the-job training, objectives should typically include the following components:

Performance:
What the employee will be able to do following the training

Conditions:
Conditions under which the performance will be attained

Criteria:
Standard or criteria of acceptable performance

Writing training objectives

Based on this information, Frank and Janet worked together to establish a training objective for Dana's position:

First draft: Answer phones and take messages.

After discussing the topic a few more minutes, they decided that the first draft was vague and needed more detail. Their second draft was clearer:

Second draft: Following on-the-job training, Dana will be able to answer the phones in a professional manner and write complete messages legibly.

Selecting Behavioral Outcomes

Research surrounding human learning has clearly documented that *"people learn by doing."* Employees need to get more involved in the on-the-job training process. Involved, not just from an activity standpoint, but also in terms of *"personal responsibility and immediate application."*

When you are selecting the most appropriate training method to use, it is often helpful to identify the type of behavioral outcomes you desire. The following guidelines provide a basic framework for deciding on potential training methods to use.

BEHAVIOR OUTCOME	DESCRIPTION	GENERAL TRAINING METHODS
Knowledge	Internalization of information	Lecture Reading Structured Discussion
Understanding	Knowledge of how to apply information on the job	Structured Discussion Case Study Personal Action Planning
Skills	Incorporation of new on-the-job behaviors	Role Play Practice Application Personal Action Planning
Attitudes and Interests	Satisfying exposure to, and demonstration of, new on-the-job behaviors	Structured Discussion Case Study Role Play Practice Application Action Planning

Seven General Training Methods

When designing on-the-job training plans, you will more than likely be concerned with, *"What is the most effective method for getting the content across to employees?"* Although there are few simple answers, it is important to consider the advantages and disadvantages of each of the seven common training methods listed below.

Lecture
One-way verbal delivery of content by the trainer

Advantages

➠ Can reinforce trainer's credibility and authority

➠ Information is concentrated and organized as desired

➠ Efficient; lots of information can be shared

➠ Can be personalized/ customized easily

Disadvantages

➠ One-way not effective if goal is shared responsibility

➠ Details get lost in the shuffle after 15-20 minutes

➠ Relative passivity of employees being trained

➠ Depends totally on trainer's effectiveness and information

➠ Usually no record of key points; comprehensiveness and consistency are suspect

➠ Words and figures can easily be garbled

Reading

Individual reading of training manuals
during a structured time frame

Advantages

➠ Gives a complete picture; all necessary details in carefully chosen words

➠ Exposes employees to large quantities of content in a concentrated time frame

➠ Learners have a good chance to study content

➠ Sketches and diagrams can be used to help

➠ Provides opportunity to review materials during and after the training experience

➠ Easily passed on to other interested parties

Disadvantages

➠ May take a lot of time to prepare

➠ Materials are competing with other references, memos, mail, etc.

➠ May seem tedious or boring to some employees

➠ Can't get immediate reaction of the learner

➠ Difficult to hold employees accountable for content; it can be forgotten or put aside

Structured Discussion

Structured conversations between employees
(*in small or large groups*), aimed toward specific learning objectives

Advantages

➠ Can explain and demonstrate at the same time

➠ Highly personal interaction among employees, and creative idea sharing

➠ Can interrupt to ask questions and clarify points

➠ Past experiences of employees contribute to the learning process

➠ Can be guided by facial expressions

➠ Can take care of brief items as they arise

Disadvantages

➠ May be dominated by a few employees

➠ Subject to interruptions and diversions

➠ Potential creation of side discussions which don't apply

➠ Can't always remember everything to cover or appropriate words

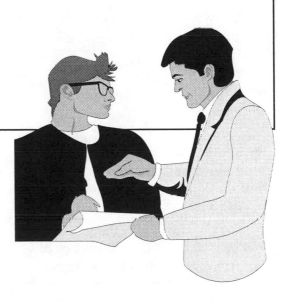

Case Study

Written description of situations that contain enough
details so employees can discuss specific recommendations

Advantages

→ Can focus the discussion
and learning experience

→ Can gain a shared
understanding of on-the-
job problems

→ Can provide *"real-world"*
applications when
customized

Disadvantages

→ May impose time limitations
for reading and discussion

→ Difficult to develop and
incorporate all the necessary
details

→ Only builds and demonstrates
understanding, not skills

Role Play

Reenactment of a specific situation by the
employees who are provided with made-up role descriptions

Advantages

→ Allows for the practice of
specific behaviors during on-
the-job training

→ Skill mastery is easier to
detect

→ Less threatening since
employees are *"playing a role"*
versus being themselves with
others

→ Can focus on the subtleties of
word choice and intonation

Disadvantages

→ Resistance of employees to
"play act" with peers

→ Key learning points may be
lost in all the action if not
properly facilitated

→ Some employees will
perceive that situations are
not *"real-world"*

→ Can be very time-
consuming

Practice Application

Immediate skill application in a specific on-the-job
situation the employees are currently facing

Advantages

➥ Practice handling a *"real-world"* situation and task using specific skills and behaviors being learned in training

➥ *"Hands-on"* experience can be more enjoyable and effective

➥ Opportunity to receive immediate coaching feedback

Disadvantages

➥ Resistance of employees to practice in front of peers

➥ Employees may often attempt to solve specific *"real-world"* situations being practiced rather than focus on skill development

➥ Some learners prefer time to digest information first instead of *"diving in"* immediately

Personal Action Planning

Identification of specific activities that employees
are committed to carry out back on the job

Advantages

➥ Immediate and focused application of skills, knowledge, or behaviors

➥ Demonstrates specific return on training investment

➥ Facilitates the documentation and reinforcement of key learnings while still at work

➥ Promotes personal accountability for learning

Disadvantages

➥ Some employees may be unwilling to make a commitment to apply training

➥ Plans may lack specific follow-up and accountability mechanisms

➥ Reinforcement may only come through punitive consequences rather than rewards

Developing on-the-job training plans

Janet considered all of the formats and ideas concerning the training for Dana. She decided that an on-the-job training plan was necessary to capture all of the details and ensure that the plan was really effective. Here is the plan Janet put together.

Employee: Dana Mills		**Training Objectives:** Following on-the-job-training, Dana will be able to answer the phones by the second ring in a professional manner and take complete, legible, hand-written messages		
Behavoiral Outcomes: Understand skills		**Training Methods:** Structured discussion, practical application, and role-playing		
WHAT	**WHO**	**HOW**	**WHEN/ WHERE**	**WHY**
• training option • specific actions/topics	• trainer • trainee(s) • evaluator	• process • resources • required time • budget • materials • equipment • staff	• schedule • location	• reasons • benefits • expectations • measurements
1. Discuss /define importance of complete and legible messages	Janet Dana	Structured discussion interview for important internal customers	Monday	Ensure Dana understands importance of message
2. Observe Dana taking messages for 30 min. Note suggestions for improvement and review messages Provide feedback	Janet Dana	Direct and objective note taking	Monday	Provide effective feedback and coaching
3. Practice taking messages for a tough call	Janet Dana	Role-play (call in)	Monday	Test new skills
4. Dana to scrutinize key learnings and methods to ensure messages are complete and legible	Janet Dana	Written summary	Tuesday	Ensure Dana has integrated learning into daily work

CHAPTER TEN WORKSHEET:
ON-THE-JOB TRAINING PLAN

Use this worksheet to develop a training plan based on identified training needs and objectives.

Employee:	Training Objectives:			
Behavioral Outcomes:	**Training Methods:**			
WHAT	**WHO**	**HOW**	**WHEN/ WHERE**	**WHY**
• training option • specific actions/topics	• trainer • trainee(s) • evaluator	• process • resources • required time • budget • materials • equipment • staff	• schedule • location	• reasons • benefits • expectations • measurements
1.				
2.				
3.				
4.				

CHAPTER ELEVEN

Summary

Providing on-the-job orientation and training for new employees is an important part of your role as a manager or supervisor. An orientation and training program gives new employees the essential information about your organization as well as the specific knowledge and skills needed to do their jobs effectively. When done poorly, on-the-job orientation and training can result in untimely resignations or long-term personnel problems. When done effectively, however, it inspires a positive work attitude within new employees, and it enables them to become productive members of your team.

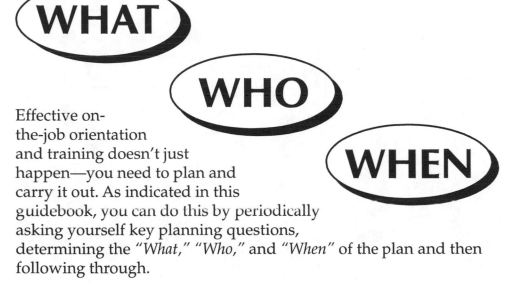

Effective on-the-job orientation and training doesn't just happen—you need to plan and carry it out. As indicated in this guidebook, you can do this by periodically asking yourself key planning questions, determining the *"What," "Who,"* and *"When"* of the plan and then following through.

You should begin by understanding your specific role in orientation and how it differs from that of the Human Resources Department in your organization. It's a good idea to meet with representatives of Human Resources to specifically define each of your roles and responsibilities.

Even though Human Resources may have an organizational orientation program, there are many things you need to initiate. The easiest way is to develop a departmental orientation checklist. This checklist should include everything a new employee may need to know about your department. It will help you to develop, implement and monitor a customized orientation and training plan, for each new employee.

Prior to the arrival of a new employee, use this guidebook to put together a plan for his or her first day. On this first day, make sure you welcome and introduce the new employee, address his or her logistical concerns, and end the day with a cordial wrap-up.

During the new employee's first week, meet with the employee and work out a specific orientation and training plan for him or her. Although this plan will eventually include long-term activities, initially focus on planning activities for this first critical week. Make time to be available to the employee during the week. At the end of the week, meet again with the employee to review progress, answer questions, and address any concerns.

Continue meeting regularly with the employee to monitor and adjust the orientation plan. Make sure you specifically review his or her progress and adjust the plan as necessary at the end of the employee's first month, sixth month, and first year.

As part of your ongoing training responsibility, conduct the following essential steps:

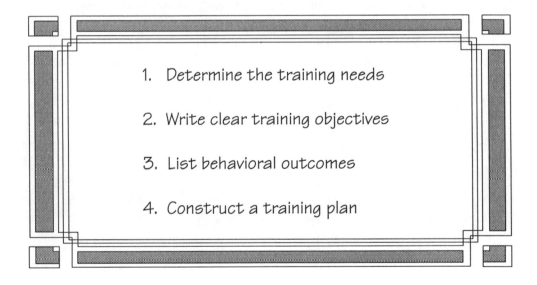

1. Determine the training needs

2. Write clear training objectives

3. List behavioral outcomes

4. Construct a training plan

Remember that constant communication, specific planning, and periodic adjusting are keys to on-the-job employee orientation and training.

REFERENCE MATERIALS
AND REPRODUCIBLE FORMS

Sample New Employee Orientation Checklist............ 100

Action Plan For Coordination 102

Practical Adult Learning Principles 103

Key Reasons Why Training Plans Succeed or Fail 105

Training Employees On Familiar Tasks 107

Training Needs Matrix 108

On-The-Job Training Plan... 109

SAMPLE NEW EMPLOYEE ORIENTATION CHECKLIST

_____   _____

New Employee's Name   **Start Date**

During the first three months of employment, the new employee's hiring supervisor and/or designated department representative should cover the following items :

Check If Done:

_____ 1. Provide essential resources and references:

____ Organizational marketing literature	____ Organizational charts
____ Product/service promotions, etc.	____ Job descriptions
____ Mission, values, philosophy, etc.	____ HR/policy manual
____ Strategic plans, goals, objectives, etc.	____ Employee handbook
____ Organizational and departmental procedures	____ Key forms, checklists, etc.

_____ 2. Review the job description and performance expectations/standards

_____ 3. Review the work schedule (include lunch, breaks, overtime, time clock, etc.)

_____ 4. Review the payroll timing, policies, and procedures

_____ 5. Review key policies:

____ Attendance/punctuality	____ Personal conduct standards
____ Sick days/leaves of absence	____ Progressive disciplinary actions
(e.g., who to notify)	____ Confidentiality
____ Holidays	____ Safety/accident procedures
____ Vacations/scheduling procedures	____ Health/first aid
____ Standard work shift	____ Emergency procedures
____ Overtime	____ Preventive maintenance
____ Performance appraisal	____ Conflict of interest
____ Wage/salary administration	____ Smoking/nonsmoking areas
____ Dress code	____ Visitors
____ Office appearance	____ Personal status changes

_____ 6. Review general administrative procedures:

____ Time cards	____ Business cards
____ Office/desk/work station keys	____ ID cards/security access
____ Calendars/schedules	____ Expense reports
____ Pertinent reports/lists	____ General supplies

_____ 7. Give introductions to members of immediate staff (include brief background of each) and other key personnel

_____ **8.** Review standard meetings to attend:

	MEETINGS	PURPOSE	MEMBERS	TIMES
a.				
b.				
c.				

_____ **9.** Give a brief tour of the surrounding area and facilities, including:

_____ Rest rooms
_____ Telephones/message systems
_____ Pay phones
_____ Mail distribution/center
_____ Copy machines/fax
_____ Bulletin boards
_____ Appointment books/schedules
_____ Time clock
_____ Computer systems/printers

_____ Equipment/tools/supplies
_____ Storage/files
_____ Books/references
_____ Break room/kitchen
_____ Coffee/vending machines
_____ Eating establishments
_____ Drinking fountains
_____ Parking
_____ Emergency exits

_____ **10.** Present initial job assignments and training plans.

	ASSIGNMENTS	TRAINING PLANS
a.		
b.		
c.		
d.		

_____ **11.** Identify coworkers (*other than the hiring supervisor*) who will train the new employee and/or act as a "buddy" to assist with general questions:

	GO TO THIS COWORKER	FOR TRAINING AND/OR ASSISTANCE REGARDING
a.		
b.		

_____ **12.** Plan for initial lunches (*designate someone to spend time with the new employee, such as a member of the management team, co-workers, and/or other employees during the first few days/weeks*)

_____ **13.** Other: _____

_____ _____ _____ _____
Hiring Supervisor's Signature **Date** **New Employee's Signature** **Date**

ACTION PLAN
FOR COORDINATION

Schedule a meeting with the Human Resources Department to determine:

➠ The role of Human Resources in the orientation program.

➠ The role of the hiring manager.

➠ How the organizational and departmental orientations will be coordinated and integrated.

❑ If you do not have a Human Resources Department that handles new employee orientation, ensure your orientation plan includes these *"general organizational"* orientation items.

❑ Contact key employees who may have interest in helping with department orientation. Share your *"vision"* of a good orientation and how they fit into that vision.

❑ Provide rewards and recognition to employees who participate in the orientation process.

❑ Assemble an *"Orientation Survival Kit"* to be used as a *"model"* for the entire company (*e.g., department administrative personnel*) when constructing a *"kit"* for new employees.

❑ Develop a process for constantly updating the orientation checklist to ensure it is continuously improved. One approach may be to ask each new employee to review the checklist and make suggestions on how to improve the list.

PRACTICAL ADULT LEARNING PRINCIPLES

Developing and conducting an effective training program should be guided by certain principles of adult learning which have been established through research by psychologists and other learning experts. Anyone training others needs to be familiar with these principles which include, but are not limited to the following:

Adults must want to learn:

❏ They strongly resist learning anything just because someone says so.

❏ It's recommended not to force them to take a training course.

Adults learn only what they feel they need to learn:

❏ They want to know, *"How is this going to help me right now?"*

❏ Train them simply and directly on what they want to know.

Adults learn only by doing:

❏ Active participation enhances the learning process.

❏ Immediate application of new knowledge or skills during training results in much higher retention.

Adults learn by solving practical problems:

❏ By incorporating customized cases and exercises, you can utilize their experience and knowledge.

❏ Application exercises should focus on real-world problems and challenges.

Adults learn through the application of past experiences:

❏ Prior experiences may make it more difficult to accept new materials and information during training.

❏ New knowledge must be related to, and integrated with, old knowledge. Providing the opportunity to interrupt, ask questions, and challenge content during training, assists in the integration with past experiences.

Adults learn best in an informal environment:

❏ Avoid reconstructing unpleasant memories of school days such as grades and assigned seating.

❏ Provide them with greater personal responsibility to measure their own progress during the training process.

Adults learn best through a variety of training methods:

❏ Learning is accomplished faster when information is presented through more than one sensory channel.

❏ A variety of training methods should be incorporated into the training approach.

KEY REASONS WHY TRAINING PLANS SUCCEED OR FAIL

Reasons For Success

1. The employee is a *"participant"* in the training process, rather than just a spectator.

2. Visible, tangible, and/or clearly understood results and expectations stimulate interest and accelerate training.

3. Employees want to see immediate job and personal benefits from training.

4. Employees want specific, real-life strategies and solutions that will satisfy their needs and interests.

5. Training plans based on past experiences and current knowledge will usually be easier to understand and retain.

6. People remember things they see more readily than those they only hear.

7. Problem-solving methods and materials are more conducive to adult learning.

8. A number of employees working together with common interests can be trained faster than the same people working alone.

9. On-the-job skill development must be used as soon as possible to be retained. What we don't use, we lose!

10. Employees learn more and at a faster pace in a positive, supportive environment. They must be free to express their viewpoints, challenge ideas, share their experiences, and learn from others, without punishment or embarrassment!

Reasons For Failure

1. The training plan is used to solve a problem that is not related to a skill deficiency:

    ⇒ Nonperformance is ignored

    ⇒ Nonperformance is rewarding

    ⇒ Performance is punished

    ⇒ Performance doesn't matter

    ⇒ Performance cannot be achieved due to obstacles

2. Training efforts are not directed at specific goals; there is no particular need for development.

3. Training objectives are not clearly defined (*e.g., the new employee is asked to "tag along" with an experienced employee as work is performed, with no learning objectives*).

4. The employee sees no perceived need or benefit.

5. The supervisor/trainer is not prepared; they don't want to train, and/or they don't have adequate knowledge of the task or basic training principles.

6. The training materials or approach are not relevant to the training goals or to the employees.

7. There is no means for receiving feedback, revising the training process, or evaluating the results.

8. There is no means for reinforcing behavior; recognition, reward, and incentive systems are absent.

TRAINING EMPLOYEES ON FAMILIAR TASKS

1. Describe the area of needed improvement.

❏ Specifically explain how/why the employee's area of needed improvement affects on-the-job performance. Cite a specific and convincing example of a project or situation where you observed this weakness.

2. Solicit the employee's ideas and perceptions.

❏ Coach the employee to analyze his own behavior and take *"ownership"* of his actions and development plans. If the employee completely denies that a problem exists, tell him that you *"perceive"* there are areas for needed improvement, and seek suggestions on how to change *your* perception.

3. React to the employee's ideas and share your own suggestions

❏ Reinforce the employee if he is *"on target,"* or redirect if he is *"off the mark,"* by sharing alternative views that will lead toward your mutual objectives

4. Seek a common development plan and summarize key steps for you and the employee to take.

❏ The more involved the employee is in discussing and resolving the area of needed improvement, the more likely he is to be committed to a plan of action.

5. Schedule a review session.

❏ Close on a positive note, communicating your confidence in the employee's success.

TRAINING NEEDS MATRIX

EMPLOYEE:	POSITION:	DATE:

RESPONSIBILITY AND SKILLS/KNOWLEDGE/ABILITIES	COMPETENCY RATING	IMPORTANCE RATING	TRAINING NEEDS

COMPETENCY RATING SCALE: 0 to 5; 0 = no experience and 5 = outstanding

IMPORTANCE RATING SCALE: 0 to 5; 0 = no importance and 5 = most importance

TRAINING NEEDS SCALE: In each row, subtract number in *"Importance Rating"* from the number in *"Competency Rating,"* *(please indicate a positive or negative number with a +/- sign)*

ON-THE-JOB TRAINING PLAN

Employee:

Training Objectives:

Behavioral Outcomes:

Training Methods:

WHAT	WHO	HOW	WHEN/ WHERE	WHY
• training option • specific actions/topics	• trainer • trainee(s) • evaluator	• process • resources • required time • budget • materials • equipment • staff	• schedule • location	• reasons • benefits • expectations • measurements
1.				
2.				
3.				
4.				
5.				

PROFESSIONAL AND PERSONAL DEVELOPMENT PUBLICATIONS FROM RICHARD CHANG ASSOCIATES, INC.

Designed to support continuous learning, these highly targeted, integrated collections from Richard Chang Associates, Inc. (RCA) help individuals and organizations acquire the knowledge and skills needed to succeed in today's ever-changing workplace. Titles are available through RCA, Jossey-Bass, Inc., fine bookstores, and distributors internationally.

PRACTICAL GUIDEBOOK COLLECTION

QUALITY IMPROVEMENT SERIES

Continuous Process Improvement
Continuous Improvement Tools, Volume 1
Continuous Improvement Tools, Volume 2
Step-By-Step Problem Solving
Meetings That Work!
Improving Through Benchmarking
Succeeding As A Self-Managed Team
Measuring Organizational Improvement Impact
Process Reengineering In Action
Satisfying Internal Customers First!

MANAGEMENT SKILLS SERIES

Interviewing And Selecting High Performers
On-The-Job Orientation And Training
Coaching Through Effective Feedback
Expanding Leadership Impact
Mastering Change Management
Re-Creating Teams During Transitions
Planning Successful Employee Performance
Coaching For Peak Employee Performance
Evaluating Employee Performance

HIGH PERFORMANCE TEAM SERIES

Success Through Teamwork
Building A Dynamic Team
Measuring Team Performance
Team Decision-Making Techniques

HIGH-IMPACT TRAINING SERIES

Creating High-Impact Training
Identifying Targeted Training Needs
Mapping A Winning Training Approach
Producing High-Impact Learning Tools
Applying Successful Training Techniques
Measuring The Impact Of Training
Make Your Training Results Last

WORKPLACE DIVERSITY SERIES

Capitalizing On Workplace Diversity
Successful Staffing In A Diverse Workplace
Team Building For Diverse Work Groups
Communicating In A Diverse Workplace
Tools For Valuing Diversity

PERSONAL GROWTH AND DEVELOPMENT COLLECTION

Managing Your Career in a Changing Workplace
Unlocking Your Career Potential
Marketing Yourself and Your Career
Making Career Transitions
Memory Tips For The Forgetful

101 STUPID THINGS COLLECTION

101 Stupid Things Trainers Do To Sabotage Success
101 Stupid Things Supervisors Do To Sabotage Success
101 Stupid Things Employees Do To Sabotage Success
101 Stupid Things Salespeople Do To Sabotage Success
101 Stupid Things Business Travelers Do To Sabotage Success

ABOUT RICHARD CHANG ASSOCIATES, INC.

Richard Chang Associates, Inc. (RCA) is a multi-disciplinary organizational performance improvement firm. Since 1987, RCA has provided private and public sector clients around the world with the experience, expertise, and resources needed to build capability in such critical areas as process improvement, management development, project management, team performance, performance measurement, and facilitator training. RCA's comprehensive package of services, products, and publications reflect the firm's commitment to practical, innovative approaches and to the achievement of significant, measurable results.

RCA RESOURCES OPTIMIZE ORGANIZATIONAL PERFORMANCE

CONSULTING — Using a broad range of skills, knowledge, and tools, RCA consultants assist clients in developing and implementing a wide range of performance improvement initiatives.

TRAINING — Practical, "real world" training programs are designed with a "take initiative" emphasis. Options include off-the-shelf programs, customized programs, and public and on-site seminars.

CURRICULUM AND MATERIALS DEVELOPMENT — A cost-effective and flexible alternative to internal staffing, RCA can custom-develop and/or customize content to meet both organizational objectives and specific program needs.

VIDEO PRODUCTION — RCA's award-winning, custom video productions provide employees with information in a consistent manner that achieves lasting impact.

PUBLICATIONS — The comprehensive and practical collection of publications from RCA supports organizational training initiatives and self-directed learning.

PACKAGED PROGRAMS — Designed for first-time and experienced trainers alike, these programs offer comprehensive, integrated materials (including selected Practical Guidebooks) that provide a wide range of flexible training options. Choose from:

- Meetings That Work! ToolPAK™
- Step-By-Step Problem Solving ToolKIT™
- Continuous Process Improvement Packaged Training Program
- Continuous Improvement Tools, Volume 1 ToolPAK™
- Continuous Improvement Tools, Volume 2 ToolPAK™
- High Involvement Teamwork™ Packaged Training Program

RICHARD
CHANG
ASSOCIATES

World Class Resources. World Class Results.^{SM}

Richard Chang Associates, Inc.
Corporate Headquarters
15265 Alton Parkway, Suite 300, Irvine, California 92618 USA
(800) 756-8096 • (949) 727-7477 • Fax: (949) 727-7007
E-Mail: info@rca4results.com • www.richardchangassociates.com

U.S. Offices in Irvine and Atlanta • Licensees and Distributors Worldwide